John G. Lake —

Apostle To Africa

by Gordon Lindsay

Published By
CHRIST FOR THE NATIONS INC.
Dallas, Texas
Reprint 2000

CONTENTS

Some Personal Memories
of Dr. John G. Lake

John Graham Lake was born at St. Mary's, Ontario, Canada, on March 18, 1870. When yet a small boy, he accompanied his parents to the United States, settling at Sault Sainte Marie, a city in northern Michigan. In October, 1891, he was admitted into the Methodist ministry at Chicago and was appointed to a church at Peshtigo, Wisconsin. However he finally decided against going there and went instead into the newspaper business. In the town of Harvey, Illinois, he founded the Harvey **Citizen**. Incidentally that town was named after D. L. Moody's brother-in-law.

In February, 1893, he married Miss Jennie Stevens of Newberry, Michigan. Three years later she was pronounced incurable of consumption by several well-known physicians who had given her the best treatment possible. They advised taking her north. On that advice Lake took her back to Sault Sainte Marie, Michigan. Two years later on April 28, 1898 she was instantly healed under the ministry of John Alexander Dowie, a story which is told later in this book.

While staying in Sault Sainte Marie, Dr. Lake opened a real estate office and took up the business of selling real estate. As a salesman and contractor he remained there until 1901. During this time he helped found the **Soo Times.** In 1904 he moved to Chicago and bought a seat on the Chicago Board of Trade. At this time he handled Jim Hill's Western Canadian land and made a personal friend of this great railroad man and financier.

The first day Lake opened his office he made $2500 on a real estate deal, and at the end of one year and nine months he had $100,000 in the bank, real estate amounting to $90,000 and also a $30,000 paid up life insurance policy. Representing the Chicago Board of Trade he met Harriman and Ryan and others who were celebrated financiers. He was employed by Ryan to form a trust of three of the nation's largest insurance companies. Appointed manager of agencies he was offered by the company a guarantee of $50,000 a year to continue in this business. It was at this point, however, that God began to deal with him in such a way that the course of his life was definitely altered. For a time he continued his work in the day hours, but at night he preached and carried on a ministry of healing.

Before we begin the fascinating story of Dr. Lake's call to

3

Africa and the amazing events which followed, the writer takes the liberty of relating some personal memories of this most unusual man. He found Christ as his Saviour in the church of which Dr. Lake was the founder. This was during the latter part of the year 1924. The career of this remarkable man of God deeply impressed him, and in no little degree influenced his ministry.

The circumstances under which the writer's parents came to attend Dr. Lake's church in Portland, Oregon, had their origin in Zion City, Illinois, during the days of Dr. John Alexander Dowie. As we have said, at that time John G. Lake was a business executive engaged in a prosperous insurance enterprise. After Dowie's death, the writer's parents moved from Zion City. At about this time, Dr. Lake also left. In the year 1908, he went to Africa as a missionary, and our family lost track of his whereabouts. However, during that time he spent five history-making years in South Africa, engaged in a ministry which in some respects rivalled that of the Early Church.

In fact, his work in Africa grew until it attracted world-wide attention. He was summoned to speak before august gatherings in which leading ministers of the world were present. He met and became intimately acquainted with many of the outstanding figures of his day, and his ministry involved an activity that brought him into international prominence in the religious world.

The healing mission at Spokane was really the climaxing work of his life. His ministry in that city became a demonstration of the power of God that resulted in over 100,000 healings during a period of five or six years. Dr. Ruthlidge of Washington, D. C. declared, "Rev. Lake through divine healing has made Spokane the healthiest city in the world, according to United States statistics." In May, 1920, Dr. Lake moved to Portland, Oregon, to found a work of similar character to that of his church in Spokane. Within a few years the work in Portland became outstanding of its kind in the state.

The writer's parents lived near Portland and upon learning that Dr. Lake had established a church in the city attended his meetings as often as they could. They took their children with them on occasions; but at that time, we regret to say, the writer was little interested in religion. However, during a revival held in that church in December, 1924, he experienced a powerful conversion to Christ. As a result, he began to attend regularly the services, which included about every day of the year. The

4

ministry of Dr. Lake, which he had some opportunity to observe during the early days of his Christian experience, was a powerful inspiration to him and indeed was to profoundly effect his future ministry.

It is an understatement to say that the ministry of John G. Lake was unusual. He possessed the remarkable ability to create faith in the hearts of his hearers. Ministers who sat under him soon found that they too had a ministry of faith that resulted in healings of a most startling character. Since it was impossible for Dr. Lake to minister personally to the great number who sought his services, he usually had a band of lay ministers and workers laboring with him to answer calls to which he was unable to attend.

One of the writer's first memories of a healing was that of a woman who was instantly healed as a result of the prayers of one of Dr. Lake's ministers. The woman was a Mrs. Watts, wife of a prominent officer of a local church. This woman had become seriously ill, and the physicians decided that her only hope was an immediate operation. The cost of the proposed operation was well beyond the family's financial resources at the time. However, in desperation the husband went to the local bank and arranged for a loan to pay for the cost of the operation. In the meantime the writer's mother, who had great faith in divine healing, felt a burden to pray for the family. She went to the sick woman and encouraged her to believe God for healing. But her church had taught against divine healing, and in fact the woman herself had not taken any interest in this teaching. But as is often the case when desperate illness or death faces one, he is inclined to alter his views. The lady consented that prayer should be offered for her healing. Mother then took the next train to Portland in hope of getting Dr. Lake to come to pray for the woman. However, when she arrived there he was not available, and as the need was urgent, mother requested that one of the other ministers go. The good brother who went did not have much of a knowledge of social amenities. In fact he was a rather rough-and-ready preacher, hardly to be distinguished for his ministerial polish. But his faith in God was strong, and though he had acquired a brusque, unceremonious manner of dealing with the sick it produced results even though his mannerisms sometimes offended people of fastidious tastes.

When mother and this preacher arrived at the home of the

5

sick woman, and he had opportunity to observe her critical condition, he lost no time in telling her that the sickness was the work of the devil. After giving the woman some instructions, he proceeded to rebuke the affliction with a loud, booming voice that carried through the whole house. Then, rather roughly, he told the woman that she was healed and for her to get out of bed. The lady at first hesitated to do this. But shortly, afraid to disobey, she did as she was told and arose from her bed to discover to her great joy that she was made whole. The pastor of the local church was at that time very much opposed to this ministry. This miracle was the first step in convincing him of its reality. Eventually, he became convinced of its Scriptural foundation and received a notable healing himself.

Incidentally, the banker who had loaned the money for the proposed operation was startled indeed a few days afterward to see the husband come to the bank to return the money. It was a testimony which caused many in the community to wonder and take note. Such were the methods used and the results obtained that gave the work of John G. Lake the prominence that it achieved.

At the time of my conversion, we were deeply impressed with this remarkable ministry that was carried on in Dr. Lake's church. During one of the first services which we attended, we observed, in a certain corner reserved for the purpose, crutches, casts, and various other paraphernalia which had been discarded by people who once had serious physical disabilities. It became evident to us that God's power was mightily in evidence in this assembly, or else there was being perpetrated one of the greatest hoaxes that the city of Portland had ever witnessed. However, after further observation and upon listening to the testimonies of those who had been healed, it was impossible for us to be otherwise than convinced of the reality of the miracles.

One of the first deliverances that we witnessed was the remarkable healing of L. C. West, a longshoreman on Portland's waterfront, who was at that time an elder in the church. (Incidentally, he supplied us with considerable material for this volume.) He was a large man who weighed over 200 pounds. While at work on the dock, a heavy object fell on his foot, crushing the bones of the ankle. An X-ray taken at the time and which he brought to the church clearly showed fractures of the bones. Consequently, he was forced to hobble about on crutches to get to the meeting.

But faith was high. We well remember the night that Brother West, after giving an account of the accident, made a public declaration that he believed the Lord would heal him. We were greatly interested in this statement, as we knew that nothing less than a miracle would make it possible for him to walk on that foot immediately, without the aid of crutches. Yet, less than a week later, he was in church again, this time without the crutches or any artificial aid, testifying to the miracle that had taken place. Such was the atmosphere of faith in the church founded by John G. Lake.

After the above incident, about a year later the writer and two other young men felt called to enter the ministry. We drove directly to San Diego where Dr. Lake was at that time ministering. He had left Portland some months before. He was kind to us and gave us the use of a tent which we set up in a neighboring community. Once a week Dr. Lake came out and preached for us. Though we did not have a large congregation to present to him, his sermons were thrilling messages of faith and we looked forward to his weekly visits with great anticipation.

At the close of our time in that city, the writer came near experiencing a sudden termination to his evangelistic career. Laid low with a most critical case of ptomaine poisoning, for days he hung between life and death. Although we earnestly looked to God for deliverance, relief did not come. We suffered excruciating pains from cramps that recurred with great intensity every few minutes. Neighbors who had taken us into their home became alarmed over what appeared to be a worsening condition and they were fearful that we would die on their hands.

Then Dr. and Mrs. Lake kindly accepted us into their home. At that time, death did not seem far off. Others believed that we would not linger more than a few hours; and indeed from the natural appearances, they were not without reason in their anticipations. Dr. Lake prayed, and although deliverance did not immediately appear, he had calm confidence that the answer had come. Mrs. Lake brought us some of the typewritten sermons of her husband, and we read these as a drowning man grasps at a straw. (These have been published under the name of THE JOHN G. LAKE SERMONS on DOMINION OVER DEMONS, DISEASE, AND DEATH.) Suddenly, faith from heaven sprang into our heart, and we arose from what many thought was a deathbed, instantly healed. It is understandable,

7

therefore, that the ministry of John G. Lake has meant a great deal to us.

At that time, Dr. Lake entertained hopes for the raising up of a chain of healing missions, on the order of his churches at Spokane and Portland. But though he had not reached advanced age, he had lived with an intensity as few men have. A decline in the strength and vitality which characterized his early ministry was apparent. It seemed he was unable to match the physical strength that was required to execute his spiritual vision. He went to Houston, Texas, and after having initial success in the founding of a church there, was called away by a message of a serious accident that almost took the life of his eldest son. He never returned to Houston.

For a time, he ministered in various churches in California. We were with him in a tent meeting at Fresno during the month of October, 1927. Later he returned to Portland, where he was pastor for a time. Afterwards, he went back to Spokane where he pastored until his death in September, 1935.

During October, 1932, we visited with Dr. Lake for the last time. On a Sunday afternoon, while we were there, he preached a message which seemed to carry much of the old-time vigor and forcefulness. It was the last message that we were ever to hear him preach.

During the week we were in Spokane, each day Dr. Lake would spend an hour or two talking to us and relating some of the great experiences he had in Africa. As Dr. Lake reminisced, it seemed to us that we were listening to an apostle of the Early Church who had walked and talked with Jesus and was recalling dramatic incidents out of the past. We listened breathlessly as he narrated instance after instance of amazing supernatural occurrences that had happened during his years of missionary work in South Africa. If we had had the foresight to take down all the notes of those wonderful hours, it would be possible to present a story which, perhaps, has had no parallel in the history of missions since the days of the Early Church. However, from here and there we have gathered fragmentary records of this great ministry and we believe that we are able to present something that will hold the interest of the reader. Perchance it may stir his heart and encourage him to launch out into new realms of faith and walk the paths reserved for those who are bold enough to believe the full witness of their God.

8

Of Dr. Lake's death, Mrs. Lake wrote: "On Labor Day, 1935, we attended a Sunday School picnic, and he came home very tired, and after a hot supper lay down to rest. A lady was speaking for us at the church, so I prevailed upon him to stay home, and I would go to church instead. When I arrived home I found that he had had a stroke while I was gone. He lingered on for two weeks being unconscious much of the time, until September 16, 1935, when he died."

In bringing these introductory remarks to a close, we add the brief testimony of Rev. B. S. Hebden, who spoke at the memorial service concerning the life and ministry of Dr. John G. Lake. It is a beautiful tribute to the unique power of this man of God:

"Mr. Lake was a strong, rugged character of loving and winning personality, and he has left his mark indelibly upon the world of gospel truth.

"Dr. Lake came to Spokane. He found us in sin. He found us in sickness. He found us in poverty of spirit. He found us in despair, but he revealed to us such a Christ as we had never dreamed of knowing this side of heaven. We thought victory was over there, but Dr. Lake revealed to us that victory was here, a present and possible reality. We regarded death almost as a friend, but Dr. Lake came and revealed to us the Christ, all glorious and all powerful, that is triumphant, compassionate, and lovely and our night was turned into day; and despair was turned into laughter. A light shone in the darkness and we, who found Christ at last as He really is, only had words as the words of Thomas who said, 'My Lord and my God.'

"How I thank God Brother Lake came to Spokane! How I thank Him that I ever contacted that man, unique, powerful! I will never forget the day in the Hutton Block when I was sick with chronic complaints, and I heard that message of Christ, that His arms were under me, and I kept it and the message kept me and, instead of my being, long and long ago, gone and forgotten I am here rejoicing and thanking our brother, Dr. Lake, who brought that message to me. Friends, he should still speak in me, not by the pen but by the Spirit that is in me, by the light that is in me, by the regeneration of Jesus Christ that is in me. Let us, friends, not go and squander it by hiding it in a napkin, but let us keep it by giving it out."

CHAPTER I

Lake's Call to the Healing Ministry

His Own Story

No one could understand the tremendous hold that the revelation of Jesus as a present day Healer took on my life, and what it meant to me, unless they understood my environment.

I was one of sixteen children. Our parents were strong, vigorous, healthy people. My mother died at the age of seventy-five, and at the present time my father still lives and is seventy-seven.

Before my knowledge and experience of the Lord as our Healer we buried eight members of the family. A strange train of sickness, resulting in death, had followed the family, and for thirty-two years some member of the family was an invalid. The home was never without the shadow of sickness during all this long period. When I think back over my boyhood and young manhood there comes to my mind remembrances like a nightmare of sickness, doctors, nurses, hospitals, hearses, funerals, graveyards and tombstones, a sorrowing household, a brokenhearted mother and grief-stricken father, struggling to forget the sorrows of the past, in order to assist the living members of the family, who needed their love and care.

At the time Christ was revealed to us as our Healer, my brother, who had been an invalid for twenty-two years, and upon whom father had spent a fortune for unavailing medical assistance, was dying. He bled incessantly from his kidneys, and was kept alive through assimilation of bloodcreating foods almost as fast as it flowed from his person. I've never know any other man to suffer so extremely and so long as he did.

A sister, thirty-four years of age, was then dying with five cancers in her left breast, having been operated on five times at Harper's Hospital, Detroit, Michigan by Dr. Karstens, a German surgeon of repute, and turned away to die. There was a large core cancer, and after the operations four other heads developed — five in all.

10

Another sister lay dying of an issue of blood. Gradually, day by day, her lifeblood flowed away until she was in the very throes of death.

I had married and established my own home. Very soon after our marriage, the same train of conditions that had followed my father's familly appeared in mine. My wife became an invalid from heart disease and tuberculosis. She would lose her heart action and lapse into unconsciousness. Sometimes I would find her lying unconscious on the floor, having been suddenly stricken, sometimes in her bed. Stronger and stronger stimulants became necessary in order to revive the action of the heart, until finally we were using nitroglycerin tablets in a final heroic effort to stimulate heart action. After these heart spells she would remain in a semi-paralytic condition for weeks, the result of over-stimulation the physicians said.

But in the midst of the deepest darkness, when baffled physicians stood back and acknowledged their inability to help, when the cloud of darkness and death was again hovering over the family, suddenly the light of God broke through into our soul, through the message of one godly minister great enough and true enough to God to proclaim the whole truth of God.

We took our brother, who was dying, to John Alexander Dowie's Healing Home in Chicago. Prayer was offered for him, with the laying on of hands, and he received an instant healing. He arose from his dying cot and walked four miles, returned to his home, and took a partnership in our father's business, a well man.

Great joy and marvelous hope sprang up in our hearts. A real manifestation of the healing power of God was before us. Quickly we arranged to take our sister with the five cancers to the same Healing Home, carrying her on a stretcher. She was taken into the healing meeting. Within her soul she said, "Others may be healed because they are good. I have not been a true Christian like others. They may be healed because of their goodness, but I fear healing is not for me." It seemed more than her soul could grasp.

After listening from her cot to the preaching and teaching of the Word of God on healing through Jesus Christ, hope sprang up in her soul. She was prayed for and hands laid on her. As the prayer of faith arose to God, the power of God descended upon her, thrilling her being. Her pain instantly vanished. The swelling disappeared gradually. The large core cancer turned black, and in a few days fell out. The smaller ones disappeared. The mutilated breast began to regrow and became a perfect breast again.

How our hearts thrilled! Words cannot tell this story. A new faith sprang up within us. If God could heal our dying brother and our dying sister, and cause cancers to disappear, He could heal anything or anybody.

THE HEALING OF THE SISTER AT DEATH'S DOOR

The sister who had the issue of blood and I had been chums from our childhood. She was a little older than I. The vision of Christ the Healer had just been opened to my soul. My mother called me one night and said, "John, if you want to see your sister alive, you must come at once." When I arrived, my mother said, "You are too late, she is gone." I stepped to her bedside and laid my hand on her forehead; it was cold and white. I slipped my hand down over her heart, and the heart had ceased to beat. I picked up a small mirror and held it over her mouth, but there was no discoloration. The breath was gone. I stood there stunned. Her husband knelt at the foot of the bed weeping. Her baby was asleep in the crib at the opposite side of the room. My old father and mother knelt sobbing at the side of the bed. They had seen eight of their children die; she was apparently the ninth. My soul was in a storm. As I looked at this sister I said, "O God, this is not your will. I cannot accept it! It is the work of the devil and darkness. It is the devil who has the power of death."

I discovered this strange fact, that there are times when one's spirit lays hold on the spirit of another. Somehow I just felt my spirit lay hold of the spirit of that sister. And I prayed, "Dear Lord, she cannot go." I walked up and down the room for some time. My spirit was crying out for somebody with faith in God that I could call upon to help me. That was twenty-five years ago when the individual who trusted God for healing was almost an insane man in the eyes of the church and the world. Bless God, it is different now. That is the advantage of having people who trust God and walk out on God's lines to come together, stay together, and form a nucleus in society which has some force for God.

As I walked up and down in my sister's room, I could think of but one man who had faith on this line. That was John Alexander Dowie, six hundred miles away. I went to the phone, called Western Union and told them I wanted to get a telegram through to Dr. Dowie with an answer back as quickly as possible. I sent this wire:

"My sister has apparently died, but my spirit will not let her go. I believe if you will pray, God will heal her."

I received this answer back:

"Hold on to God. I am praying. She will live."

I have asked a thousand times, "What would it have meant if instead of that telegram of faith, I had received one from a weakling preacher who might have said, 'I am afraid you are on the wrong track,' or 'Brother you are excited,' or 'The days of miracles are past'?"

It was the strength of his faith that came over the wire that caused the lightnings of my soul to begin to flash, and while I stood at the telephone and listened, the very lightnings of God began to flash in my spirit. I prayed, "This thing is of hell; it cannot be; it will not be. In the Name of Jesus Christ, I abolish this death and sickness, and she shall live." And as I finished praying, I turned my eyes toward the bed, and I saw her eyelids blink. But I was so wrought up I said, "Maybe I am deceiving myself." So I stood a little while at the telephone, the lightnings of God still flashing through my soul. Presently I observed her husband get up and tiptoe to her head, and I knew that he had seen it. I said, "What is it Peter?" He replied, "I thought I saw her eyelids move." And just then they moved again. Five days later she came to father's home and sat down with us to Christmas dinner, the first time in their life when the Lake family was all well.

THE HEALING OF HIS INVALID WIFE

My wife, who had been slowly dying for years, and suffering untold agonies, was the last of the four to receive God's healing touch. But, oh ere God's power came upon her I realized as I never had before the character of consecration God was asking and that a Christian should give to God. Day by day, death silently stole over her, until the final hours had come. A brother minister was present. He stood by her bedside, then returning me with tears in his eyes, said, "Come and walk." And together we strolled out into the moonlight. He said to me, "Brother Lake, be reconciled to the will of God," meaning by that as most all ministers do, "Be reconciled to let your wife die." I thought of my babies. I thought of her whom I loved as my own soul, and

13

a flame burned in my heart. I felt as if God had been insulted by such a suggestion. Yet, I had many things to learn.

In the midst of my soul storm I returned to my home, picked up my Bible from the mantelpiece, threw it on the table. And if ever God caused a man's Bible to open to a message that his soul needed, surely He did then for me. The book opened at the tenth chapter of Acts, and my eyes fell on the thirty-eighth verse, which read: "Jesus of Nazareth with the Holy Ghost and power: who went about doing good, and healing all that were oppressed of the DEVIL; for God was with him."

Like a flash from the blue these words pierced by heart. "Oppressed of the devil!" Then God was not the author of sickness, and the people whom Jesus healed had not been made sick by God! Hastily taking a reference to another portion of the Word, I read again from the words of Jesus in Luke 13:16, "Ought not this woman . . . whom SATAN HATH BOUND, lo, these eighteen years, be loosed from this bond?" Once again Jesus attributed sickness to the devil. What a faith sprang up in my heart, and what a flame of intelligence concerning the Word of God and the ministry of Jesus went over my soul. I saw as never before why Jesus healed the sick. He was doing the will of His Father, and in doing His Father's will was **destroying the works of the devil.** (Heb. 2:14.)

In my soul I said, "This work of the devil, this destruction of my wife's life, in the name of Jesus Christ shall cease, for **Christ died and Himself took our infirmities and bore our sicknesses.**"

We decided on 9:30 a.m., as an hour when prayer should be offered for her recovery, and again I telephoned and telegraphed friends to join me in prayer at that hour. At 9:30, I knelt at her dying bed and called on the living God. The power of God came upon her, thrilling her from head to foot. Her paralysis was gone, her heart became normal, her cough ceased, her breathing was regular, her temperature was normal. The power of God was flowing through her person, seemingly like the blood flows through the veins. As I prayed I heard a sound from her lips. Not the sound of weakness as formerly, but now a strong, clear voice, and she cried out, "Praise God, I am healed!" With that, she caught the bedclothing, threw them back from her, and in a moment was out on the floor.

What a day! Shall I ever forget it, when the power of God

14

thrilled our souls, and the joy of God possessed our hearts at her recovery?

The news spread throughout the city and the state, and the nation. The newspapers discussed it. Our home became a center of inquiry. People traveled for great distances to see her and to talk with her. She was flooded with letters of inquiry.

A great new light had dawned in our soul. Our church had diligently taught us that the days of miracles were past. Believing thus, eight members of the family had been permitted to die. But now, with the light of truth flashing in our hearts, we saw that such teaching was a lie, no doubt invented by the devil, and diligently heralded as truth by the church, thus robbing mankind of his rightful inheritance through the blood of Jesus.

Others came to our home. They said, "Since God has healed you, surely He will heal us. Pray for us." We were forced into it. God answered, and many were healed. Many years have passed since then, but no day has gone by in which God has not answered prayer. People have been healed, not by ones and twos, nor by hundreds, or even thousands, but by tens of thousands. For I have devoted my life, day and night, to this ministry.

CHAPTER II

How God Sent John G. Lake to Africa

Eight years passed after God revealed Jesus the Healer to me. I had been practicing the ministry of healing. During that eight years every answer to prayer, every miraculous touch of God, every response of my own soul to the Spirit had created within me a more intense longing for an intimacy and a consciousness of God, like I felt the disciples of Jesus and the primitive church had possessed.

HE RECEIVES SPECIAL ANOINTING OF THE SPIRIT

Shortly after my entrance into the ministry of healing, while attending a service where the necessity for the Baptism of the Spirit was presented, as I knelt in prayer and reconsecration to God, an anointing of the Spirit came upon me. Waves of Holy Glory passed through my being, and I was lifted into a new realm of God's presence and power. After this, answers to prayer were frequent and miracles of healing occurred from time to time. I felt myself on the borderland of a great spiritual realm, but was unable to enter in fully, so my nature was not satisfied with the attainment.

Finally I was led to set aside certain hours of the day that I dedicated to God, as times of meditation and prayer. Thus a number of months passed, until one morning as I knelt praying the Spirit of the Lord spoke within my spirit, and said, "Be patient until autumn." My heart rejoiced in this encouragement and I continued my practice of meditation and prayer as formerly. It became easy for me to detach myself from the course of life, so that while my hands and mind were engaged in the common affairs of every day, my spirit maintained its attitude of communion with God.

At this time in addition to my work as minister of the Gospel,

I was engaged as a manager of agents for a life insurance company. During the period of which I speak, I preached practically every night. After the services I was in the habit of joining a circle of friends who like myself were determined to pray through into God where we could receive the Baptism of the Holy Ghost, as we believed the early disciples had received it. I said, "God, if you will baptize me in the Holy Spirit, and give me the power of God, nothing shall be permitted to stand between me and a hundred-fold obedience."

HOW I RECEIVED THE BAPTISM OF THE HOLY GHOST

I prayed for the Baptism of the Holy Ghost for nine months, and if a man ever prayed honestly and sincerely in the faith, I did. Finally one day I was ready to throw up my hands and quit. I said, "Lord, it may be for others, but it is not for me. You just cannot give it to me." I did not blame God.

One night a gentleman by the name of Pierce said, "Mr. Lake, I have been wishing for a long time you would come over and we would spend a night in prayer together. We have been praying for the Baptism for a whole year and there is not one of us baptized yet. Brother, I do not believe that you are either, so we can pray for one another." I was so hungry to pray, so I went with all the intentions of praying for the rest, but I had not been praying five minutes until the light of God began to shine around me. I found myself in a center of an arc of light ten feet in diameter — the whitest light in all the universe. So white! O how it spoke of purity. The remembrance of that whiteness, that wonderful whiteness, has been the ideal that has stood before my soul, of the purity of the nature of God ever since.

A VOICE SPOKE OUT OF THE VISION OF LIGHT

Then a Voice began to talk to me out of that light. There was no form. And the Voice began to remind me of this incident and that incident of disobedience to my parents, from a child; of my obstinacy, and dozens of instances when God brought me up to the line of absolutely putting my body, soul and spirit upon the altar forever. I had my body upon the altar for ten years, and I had been a minister of the Gospel. But when the Lord comes, He opens to the soul the depths that have never been touched in your life. Do you know that after I was bap-

17

tized in the Holy Ghost, things opened up in the depths of my nature that had remained untouched in all my life, and that which was shadowy, distant, and hazy became real. God got up close and let His light shine into me.

Shortly after this experience, one afternoon a brother minister called and invited me to accompany him to visit a lady who was sick. Arriving at the home we found the lady in a wheel chair. All her joints were set with inflammatory rheumatism. She had been in the condition for ten years.

While my friend was conversing with her, preparing her to be prayed with that she might be healed, I sat in a deep chair on the opposite side of a large room. My soul was crying out to God in a yearning too deep for words, when suddenly it seemed to me that I had passed under a shower of warm tropical rain, which was not falling upon me but through me. My spirit and soul and body under this influence soothed into such a deep still calm as I had never known. My brain, which had always been so active, became perfectly still. An awe of the presence of God settled over me. I knew it was God.

Some moments passed; I do not know how many. The Spirit said, "I have heard your prayers, I have seen your tears. You are now baptized in the Holy Spirit." Then currents of power began to rush through my being from the crown of my head to the soles of my feet. The shocks of power increased in rapidity and voltage. As these currents of power would pass through me, they seemed to come upon my head, rush through my body and through my feet into the floor. The power was so great that my body began to vibrate intensely so that I believe if I had not been sitting in such a deep low chair I might have fallen upon the floor.

At that moment I observed my friend was motioning me to come and join him in prayer for the woman who was sick. In this absorption he had not noticed that anything had taken place in me. I arose to go to him, but I found my body trembling so violently that I had difficulty in walking across the room, and especially in controlling the trembling of my hands and arms. I knew that it would not be wise to thus lay my hands upon the sick woman as I was likely to jar her. It occurred to me that all that was necessary was to touch the tips of my fingers on the top of the patient's head and then the vibrations would not jar her. This I did. At once the currents of holy power passed through my being, and I knew that it likewise passed through the one that was sick. She did not speak, but apparently was amazed at the effect in her body.

My friend who had been talking to her in his great earnestness had been kneeling as he talked to her. He arose saying, "Let us pray that the Lord will now heal you." As he did so he took her by the hand. At the instant their hands touched, a flash of dynamic power went through my person and through the sick woman, and as my friend held her hand the shock of power went through her hand into him. The rush of power into his person was so great that it caused him to fall on the floor. He looked up at me with joy and surprise and springing to his feet said, "Praise the Lord, John, Jesus has baptized you in the Holy Ghost!"

Then he took the crippled hand, that had been set for so many years. The clenched hands opened, and the joints began to work, first the fingers, then the hand and the wrist, then the elbow and shoulder.

These were the outward manifestations. But Oh! who could describe the thrills of joy inexpressible that were passing through my spirit? Who could comprehend the peace and presence of God that thrilled my soul? Even at this late date, the awe of that hour rests upon my soul. My experience has truly been as Jesus said that He shall be within you "a well of water, springing up into everlasting life." That never-ceasing fountain has flowed through my spirit, soul and body day and night, bringing salvation and healing and the Baptism of the Spirit in the power of God to multitudes.

THE RESULT OF THE HOLY SPIRIT BAPTISM

Shortly after my Baptism in the Holy Spirit, a working of the Spirit commenced in me, that seemed to have for its purpose the revelation of the nature of Jesus Christ to me and in me. Through this tuition and remolding of the Spirit a great tenderness for mankind was to awaken in my soul. I saw mankind through new eyes. They seemed to me as wandering sheep, having strayed far, in the midst of confusion, groping and wandering hither and thither. They had no definite aim and did not seem to understand what the difficulty was or how to return to God.

The desire to proclaim the message of Christ, and demonstrate His power to save and bless, grew in my soul until my life was swayed by this overwhelming passion.

THE CALL VERSUS BUSINESS INTERESTS

However, my heart was divided. I could not follow successfully the ordinary pursuits of life and business. When a man came into my office, though I knew that twenty or thirty minutes of concentration on the business in hand would possibly net me thousands of dollars, I could not discuss business with him. By a new power of discernment I could see his soul, understand his inner life and motives. I recognized him as one of the wandering sheep, and longed in an overwhelming desire to help him get to God for salvation and to find himself.

I determined to discuss the matter with the president of my company. I frankly told him the condition of soul in which I found myself and its cause. He kindly replied, "You have worked hard, Lake. You need a change. Take a vacation for three months, and if you want to preach, preach. But at the end of three months $50,000.00 a year will look like a lot of money to you, and you will have little desire to sacrifice it for the dreams of religious possibilities."

I thanked him, accepted an invitation to join a brother in evangelistic work, and left the office, never to return.

During the three months, I preached every day to large congregations, saw a multitude of people saved from their sins and healed of their diseases, and hundreds of them baptized in the Holy Ghost. At the end of three months, I said to God, "I am through forever with everything in life but the proclamation and demonstration of the Gospel of Jesus Christ."

I disposed of my estate and distributed my funds in a manner I believed to be in the best interests of the Kingdom of God, and made myself wholly dependent upon God for the support of myself and my family, and abandoned myself to the preaching of Jesus.

THE CALL TO AFRICA

While ministering in a city in Northern Illinois, the chore boy at the hotel where we were stopping was inquiring for someone to assist him in sawing down a large tree. I volunteered to assist him, and while in the act of sawing down the tree, the Spirit of the Lord spoke within my spirit clear and distinctly,

"Go to Indianapolis. Prepare for winter campaign. Get a large hall. In the Spring you will go to Africa."

I went to Indianapolis. The Lord directed me in a marvelous way, so that in a few days I had secured a large hall and was conducting services as He directed. About this time the following incident took place, which has had so much to do with the success of my ministry ever since.

HE RECEIVES POWER TO CAST OUT DEMONS

One morning when I came down to breakfast I found my appetite had disappeared. I could not eat. I went about my work as usual. At dinner I had no desire to eat, and no more in the evening. This went on till the third day. But toward the evening of the third day an overwhelming desire to pray took possession of me. I wanted only to be alone to pray. Prayer flowed from my soul like a stream. I could not cease praying. As soon as it was possible to get a place of seclusion I would kneel to pour out my heart to God for hours. Whatever I was doing, that stream of prayer continued flowing from my soul.

On the night of the sixth day of this fast that the Lord had laid on me, while in the act of washing my hands, the Spirit said to me once again, "Go and pray." I turned around and knelt by my bedside. As I knelt praying, the Spirit said, "How long have you been praying to cast out demons?" and I replied, "Lord a long time." And the Spirit said, "From henceforth thou shalt cast out demons." I arose and praised God.

THE CASE OF THE DEMON-POSSESSED MAN

The following night at the close of the service a gentleman came to me, and pointing to a large red-letter motto on the wall, which read, "In my name shall they cast out devils," he asked, "Do you believe that?" I replied, "I do." He said, "Do not answer hastily, for I have gone around the land seeking for a minister who would tell me he believed that. Many said that they did, but when I questioned them I found they wanted to qualify the statement." I said, "Brother, so far as I know my soul, I believe it with all my heart."

Then he continued, "I will tell you why I asked. Two and one-half years ago my brother who was a manager of a large elevator became violently insane. He was committed to the asylum and is there today. Somehow he became possessed of an evil spirit. Physicians who have examined him declare that every function of his body and brain are apparently normal, and they cannot account for his insanity." I replied, "Brother, bring him on."

On Sunday in the midst of the service, the man came, attended by the brother, the mother, and an attendant of the institution. I stopped preaching, selected a half dozen persons who I knew were people who had faith in God to join me in prayer for his deliverance. I stepped from the platform, laid my hands on his head, and in the Name of Jesus Christ, the Son of God, commanded the devil that possessed him to come out of him. The Spirit of God went through my being like a flash of lightning. I knew in my soul that the evil spirit was cast out, and was not surprised when in a moment the man raised his head and spoke intelligently to me. A few days later he was discharged from the institution, returned home a healed man and resumed his former position as manager of a grain elevator.

Thus God verified His word to me, and from that day to this, the power of God has remained upon my soul, and I have seen hundreds of insane people delivered and healed.

MONEY COMES TO PROVIDE PASSAGE TO AFRICA

One day during the following February my preaching partner said to me, "John, how much will it cost to take our party to Johannesburg, South Africa?" I replied, "Two thousand dollars." He said, "If we are going to Africa in the Spring, it is time you and I were praying for the money." I said, "I have been praying for the money ever since New Year. I have not heard from the Lord or anyone else concerning it." He added, "Never mind, let's pray again." A few days later he returned from the post office and threw out upon the table four $500 drafts saying, "John, there is the answer. Jesus has sent it. We are going to Africa."

We left Indianapolis on the first day of April, 1908, my wife and I and seven children and four others. We had our tickets to Africa but no money for personal expenses en route except $1.50. (At this point in the narrative Dr. Lake relates several remarkable providences of God which supplied their expenses en route.)

Through my knowledge of the immigration laws of South Africa, I knew that before we would be permitted to land, I must show the immigration inspector that I was possessor of at least $125.00 We prayed earnestly over this matter, and about the time we reached the equator a rest came into my soul concerning it. I could pray no more.

About eight or ten days later we arrived in Cape Town harbor, and our ship anchored. The immigration inspector came on board and the passengers lined up at the purser's office to present their money and receive their tickets to land. My wife asked, "What are you going to do?" I said, "I am going to line up with the rest. We have obeyed God thus far. It is now up to the Lord. If they send us back we cannot help it."

As I stood in line awaiting my turn, a fellow passenger touched me on the shoulder and indicated to me to step out of line, and come over to the ship's rail to speak with him. He asked some questions, and then drew from his pocket a traveler's checkbook, and handed me two money orders aggregating $200.00. I stepped back into line, presented my orders to the inspector and received our tickets to land.

GOD PROVIDES THEM A HOME IN AFRICA

Johannesburg is one thousand miles inland from Cape Town. Throughout the voyage and on the train we earnestly prayed about the subject of a home. We were faith missionaries. We had neither a board nor friends behind us to furnish money. We were dependent on God. Many times during the trip to Johannesburg we bowed our heads and reminded God that when we arrived there, we should need a home. God blessed and wondrously answered our prayer.

Upon our arrival at Johannesburg I observed a little woman bustling up. She said, "You are an American missionary party?" The reply was, "Yes." Addressing me she said, "How many are there in your family?" I answered, "My wife, myself and seven children." "O," she said, "you are the family. The Lord has sent me to meet you, and I want to give you a home."

That same afternoon we were living in a furnished cottage in the suburbs, the property of our beloved benefactor, Mrs. C. L. Goodenough, of Johannesburg, who remains to this day our beloved friend and fellow worker in the Lord.

CHAPTER III
Historic Revival in South Africa

(The story of the epic revival in South Africa would fill many volumes if it could be fully told. We have to pick up the thread of the story from different sources. We are deeply indebted to W. F. Burton who has kindly given us permission to use this material from his book **When God Makes a Pastor.**)

In April, 1908, a party of Spirit-filled men and women called of God set out from Indianapolis, to carry the full gospel to South Africa.

Though seventeen started, a number of them stayed in England, on the way out and only Mr. and Mrs. Lake, with their children, Mr. and Mrs. Hezmelhalch, Mr. Lehman and a Miss Sackett arrived in Johannesburg, at the commencement of the work. A number of other workers followed later.

Tom Hezmelhalch had been a preacher in the American Holiness Church and had joined Lake in a successful evangelistic campaign in Zion City just prior to their sailing.

John Lake had been an elder in the Zion Apostolic Church when Dowie was at the height of his power. He was a man of strong, forceful personality, who would have made his way to the fore in any situation. On leaving America, he left behind him a successful business, arranging for his brother to settle his affairs. Also Hezmelhalch had had land in California, but sold it in order to leave for Africa unencumbered.

Lehman was the only one of the party who had previously visited Africa. He had been preaching to the natives for five years and was able to speak in Zulu.

There was absolutely no organization behind these men. A friend gave them two thousand dollars at the last moment, but it did not go very far with a party of seventeen, though they were able to secure tickets all the way from Indianapolis to Johannesburg for the ridiculously small sum of twenty-five pounds each.

Lake had known Overseer Bryant, of the Zion Apostolic Church in South Africa, and this elder had urged his flock to seek a deeper experience in God, and to pray to be baptized in the Holy Ghost. He had thus to some extent prepared the way for revival that followed. Bryant, however, had been recalled by Dowie and had actually passed this first party on the high seas.

From the very start it was as though a spiritual cyclone had struck Doornfontein. Before many weeks, scores were saved and filled with the Holy Spirit, and hundreds were healed.

A little boy of four years old had been given up by four doctors. The poor little fellow had a hopeless curvature of the spine, but within two weeks of his being prayed for, he was absolutely healed.

One man of desperately bad character, a spiritualist, came under conviction of sin and found his way into the hall. Soon he heard an audible voice telling him, "Go and ask Lake to pray for you." Leaping over the prostrate natives about him, he went forward and said, "Man of God, God says you must pray for me." Lake and Hezmelhalch placed their hands on him, and in a minute he was saved, filled with the Holy Spirit, and praising God in new tongues.

Among others who had entered the hall was the governess of Johannesburg's chief Jewish Rabbi, and she was amazed to hear this ex-spiritualist extolling the Lord in pure Hebrew.

His brother, a stationmaster, was believed to be a man of irreproachable character; and he too became hungry. However, though he prayed and pleaded with God for blessing, nothing happened. He became desperate and began to realize that he must make a clean breast of much secret sin in his life.

At last in a meeting which lasted till four in the morning, the stationmaster drew from his pockets a watch and handful of money, placing these on one side, and within a few minutes he was filled with the Holy Spirit. Those present recognized the German language. Afterwards it transpired that the money he had set aside was some of which he had taken from natives, by charging them more than was just for their tickets, while the watch had fallen out of somebody's suitcase; and instead of returning it, he had kept it. Since the stolen property could not be returned to its owners, it was handed to the evangelists for their work.

A feature of the work was the demonstrations of answered prayer. A woman had been deserted by her husband, a prominent retired government official. She had no idea where he was, but asked prayer that God would bring him back and save him from drink. This man was away in another part of the country but at the very time prayer was offered, he was smitten with such conviction that in three days he was home; and better still he was delivered from drink and saved by the power of God.

In this way, prayer offered in Johannesburg was answered away in the Free State of Natal, so that the news spread like wildfire and people came seeking God from distant parts of the country.

Many were so hungry that though the meetings ended late, they would accompany the preachers to their homes to talk and ask more about the things of God. Often the day broke and still they were teaching, answering questions and praying for the sick. In the daytime it was even better. One would find people on the tramcars and in the streets, with their Bibles, talking about these wonderful miracles and showing each other the scriptural foundation for such works.

At times the crush was so great, and the sick needing prayer were so many that Mrs. Lake had no time to prepare the food. Indeed they had to arrange to usher the people in at the front door, pray for them as they went through the house, and then show them out at the back to make room for more.

Among the earliest homes to open for meetings and to help the work and workers were those of the families of Vander Byl and Stuart. These people had been connected with the Christian Catholic Apostolic Church in Zion and were hungry for God's best at any price. When the little hall at Doornfontein became hopelessly small, fifteen simultaneous cottage meetings were arranged in different parts of the town with a big central "power-house" prayer meeting at the Schuman home.

All this was settled, however, and as they ministered together, it was wonderful to see the perfect understanding which each had of the other. Often if Lake were preaching, Hezmelhalch would step forward, and say, "Wait a bit, John, and let me explain that point."

Then, a few minutes later, Lake would call, "Now, hold on a while, Brother Tom, while I clinch that point."

In this way frequently each would speak five or six times

in the course of a meeting, and nobody could tell actually where the one message ended and the other began. It was all one ministry in the Spirit.

At this time much of the Rand mine labour was done by Chinamen. Now it happened that a big Chinaman, whom nobody seemed to know by any other name than that of John, had come all the way from China, entirely trusting God to supply his needs that he might evangelize among his fellow-countrymen in the mines. He was a fine, intelligent man, and spoke English well, while he was much respected for his integrity and evident sincerity of purpose.

The missionary John Ingham brought John along to the meetings to see and hear for himself. There was much that was new and amazing to the Chinaman, and his mind was in a quandary as to whether this was really of God or not. Thus he lifted his heart to God to show him very clearly and unmistakably whether it was His work.

A moment later a litle girl stood before him, and said, "This work is of God." Moreover she said this in perfect Chinese. This was a threefold miracle. It was miraculous that she should have been led directly to him. It was equally amazing that she should have answered the very question that was in his heart. Moreover it was more wonderful still that she should address him perfectly in a language she had never learned.

So impressed was John the Chinaman with this that he asked God to fill him too with the Holy Spirit, and after receiving the Comforter, he went back to carry the good news to his own people in China.

The demonstrations of healing at this time, stirred not only Johannesburg, but the country at large. The sick would come up on to the platform on one side, weak and suffering, and would go off the other side shouting, "God has healed me," at the same time leaving their crutches and trusses behind, while the crowd cheered and shouted with joy.

Almost all the Christian Catholic Apostolic Church in Johannesburg came into this great blessing, though those at Pretoria held aloof. However the brothers were now asked to hold meetings in the Zion Church in Bree Street. It was a commodious building, holding some six hundred.

Soon the revival tide was rising at Bree Street. Not a meeting passed without the demonstration of the Spirit's power. A deaf and dumb child brought from Potschefstroom was healed as the people looked on. He declared later that he saw Jesus come and touch his ears and tongue. For a time he was quite bewildered at the noise he heard around him for the first time in his life.

Once after an inspired address almost the whole congregation moved forward to the penitent form, when a big man fell near the front in an epileptic seizure. Like a flash Lake was off the platform, and at his side, rebuking the demon in the name of Jesus, and then he quietly returned to the platform. But the work was done. The fit was cut short, and the man never had another.

God was at work mightily, but so was the devil. At times pandemonium reigned, and while the people were being saved and blessed in the front of the hall, godless opposers were shrieking and jeering at the back.

One night two men brought bulldogs to the back of the hall, to create a panic, but instead of the dogs interfering with the people they went at each other. This so enraged their owners that they too rushed at each other, and eventually withdrew without having done anything but harm each other.

Another night a woman struggled up to the platform on crutches and told Lake that she had been to Johannesburg's best doctors, but was none the better. She was now under treatment from a hypnotist.

"Where is the man now?" asked Lake.

"He is there in the front," she answered.

Lake stepped to the front of the platform, and thundered, "You hypnotic devil, come out of him," and then later, "and never enter into him any more."

The man made good his escape as soon as possible, and the woman stepped off the platform, perfectly healed.

Next day the man was back, pleading, "Lake, I will give you a big sum of money if you will give me back my power to hypnotize."

Lake told him, "Man, I didn't take it away. God took it from you. Thank Him that you are rid of it. You will never hypnotize another man as long as you live, so go and earn an honest living."

Few people understood the meaning of living by faith, and as there were no collections, the preachers and their families often went hungry. They were so big-hearted that they would

28

pick up drunken men off the streets, and take them home, clean them up, and get them saved.

One drug addict had several sons all of whom came into the light. They prayed for him, but he did not get deliverance. Then Lake said that he would like all the sons to spend the night with him, in prayer and fasting for their father's deliverance, and before morning the accursed craving for drugs had left him forever, and he was a saved man.

This man had a farm in the Northern Transvaal, and it was thus that the news of this great revival reached that part of the country.

Many people from other denominations came to be healed and to be filled with the Holy Spirit, carrying the testimony back to their churches.

On one occasion two young women came to the back of the hall to scoff and create a disturbance. Suddenly one was struck down as by an unseen hand, and fell to the floor, apparently dead. Whereupon her sister went to call Lake, saying, "Man of God, we have sinned, but forgive us and restore my sister."

Lake prayed for her. She was raised up at once, and both the young women were soundly converted.

So mightily did the power of God rest upon the preachers at this time that even as Lake shook hands with the people, on entering the hall, they would fall to the ground, under the Spirit's unction.

On one occasion a brother came asking for prayer on behalf of his sister, who was in a lunatic asylum in England. Later it was proved, that at the very moment they prayed in the Bree Street Hall, the woman was instantly and completely delivered from insanity in England.

Of course the opposers of the truth credited all this to hypnotism, though we have already seen how opposed was Lake's attitude to the hypnotist.

However, an enraged mob entered the back of the hall one night, with pick handles and other weapons, saying what they were going to "do for that hypnotist."

The preachers continued their service as though there were nothing wrong, and at the end Lake walked quietly and lovingly up to the men who were waiting to brain him, holding out his hand, and saying, "God bless you." He walked through the midst of them, and not a soul could lift his hand to do him harm.

The whole revival at this time was so intensely dramatic that it would be difficult to describe the thousands who were saved and the amazing healings which took place by scores.

Lake's name was on everyone's lips. One day he was passing a crowd that stood about a fallen horse. The poor animal had been struck by the shaft of a passing cart, and was bleeding to death. Someone saw Lake and shouted, "Why doesn't this man do something for it?"

Lake took this as a challenge, and stepping up to the horse, removed his hat, and signalled the crowd for silence. Then kneeling, he placed his hand over the spot from which the blood was pouring, and simply said, "In the mighty name of the Lord Jesus Christ."

After this he quietly made his way through the crowd, and was gone, but a moment later the bleeding stopped and the horse stood on its feet.

One of the many who flocked to Bree Street to investigate was a keen member of the Johannesburg Criminal Investigation Department, as smart a body of men as one could meet.

This man was well acquainted with the "crooks" and criminals of the town, and to his amazement he saw the worst of them coming night after night. Here was a wife-beater, there a buyer of stolen gold. Diamond smugglers, and illicit liquor runners, burglars, touts for the houses of ill fame, harlots. and "drunks" —they flocked to the penitent forms and became new creatures in Christ Jesus.

"Hello! Charlie, they tell me you are going to the mad folk."

The man addressed was struggling along the street on crutches. As a boy he had been struck on the head by a stone from a catapult. Later his hand had been caught in a machine, cutting the tendons of the wrist, and finally his foot and leg had been irreparably damaged under the fall of a heavy pulley. His wife had struggled to keep the home together for him and for the baby girl. Often his ears and nose would run with offensive pus. The hand hung loose and helpless and after months in a hospital the Johannesburg doctors had discharged him as incurable. The poor man had contemplated suicide, for it seemed as though he were useless and a drag upon his noble wife.

Day after day she worked to keep their wee home intact, and now at last a new hope had dawned as they heard of healing for everyone who would come to Jesus.

"Yes!" answered Charlie. "I'm going to the mad people, and what's more I believe that I shall soon walk and work again."

That night his wife went to bed, tired out, while Charlie went to the meeting. As the invitation was given, a great faith rose in his heart, and he limped forward to the platform. They anointed him, and a moment later the power of God went through his being like a flame, and he found that he was healed. The crowd cheered, and Charlie went running and jumping home to tell his wife.

She was awakened by someone vaulting backwards and forwards across the table. She went cold with fear, thinking that a drunken native must have found his way into the house. Opening her door very cautiously, she peered through the chink into the dining room, and to her amazement she saw her husband, who a couple of hours before had left the house on crutches, now healed and delirious with delight and shouting glory to Jesus.

The crutches had been left behind. He had no further need for them, and the next day the man who had jeered at Charlie for "going to the mad people," saw him walking boldly down the street, on a perfectly sound pair of legs, while shortly afterwards his head and hand were also healed by the Lord.

It is strange to realize that during this time with thousands being saved and healed, the little missionary party was often in the direst need. It is true that some faithful souls would occasionally leave a basket of food at the door, or help with clothing for the big Lake family. Yet on the whole the people did not think of the supplies, believing that Lake must be supported by some society overseas.

Then one day a lady was led to call Mrs. Lake aside and to put ten shillings into her hand, apologizing that it was so small a sum.

"Small!" remarked Mrs. Lake, "why even a tickey (a threepenny bit) would be welcome." They had not a penny in the house.

A few months later Mrs. Lake died. The splendid woman had literally given her life for the work. Again and again that noble pair had put their hands into their pockets, and given their last half crown to some poor soul whom they considered more needy, or less able to trust God than they.

People were saved thousands of pounds in doctors' fees, and even better; they were restored in health and limb, in a way which meant more to them than priceless gold; yet few ever thought of giving the preachers a helping hand.

Meetings were held successively in a Hebrew school, a picture house, and a motor training college, all of which meant the paying of heavy rents, so that those outside the little band thought that the preachers must have large resources or they could not maintain such places. All the while greater and more dramatic miracles were seen.

A man named Swanepoel was working down in one of the Rand gold mines, when a blasting cartridge discharged prematurely, knocking him backwards and bursting his eye. He was carried to the hospital where the doctors declared that the remains of the eye must be removed at once.

However, Swanepoel had heard of the remarkable answers to prayer in Lake's meetings and asked if he might be taken to John Lake before he decided to have the eye removed. He was warned that a delay might not only involve the eye, but might even mean his death. However he was taken to Lake in an agony of suffering. Lake helped him out of the cab, and took him for prayer into a room where a few Christians were gathered. The bandage was removed, and as prayer was offered, one of those present looked curiously into the face of the suffering man. To his amazement he saw the scattered fragments of the eye gradually draw together as by an unseen hand, and by the time "Amen" was uttered, the eye was once more perfect and the pain gone!

Swanepoel at once returned to the hospital and showed the doctors a perfect pair of eyes.

On one occasion they were called to the bedside of a dying girl, Miss Maggie Truter. By the time they reached her, life was practically extinct. However, the workers gave themselves to prayer. For some hours nothing happened. Some of the Christians present were overcome by unbelief and left, even telling Lake that it was useless and heartless to continue to raise false hopes in the relatives. Life had gone. The body was stiff and cold. They must own up that they had failed.

Nevertheless, Lake's soul was filled with a mighty faith, and a conviction that the deliverance of this girl would be for the glory of the Lord Jesus and the vindication of His Word. Thus he prayed on, till those stood looking on declared that they saw pallor give way to freshness and warmth. Presently the body stirred. Maggie Truter sat up, and to the time of the writing of this report some twenty-five years later, she is still living, a miraculous testimony to the power of the name of our Lord Jesus Christ.

Let it be fairly stated, however, that soul healing was always given the preference to the healing of the body. The taking away of nature's infirmities was always held as subsidiary to the taking away of sin. Old debts were paid, restitution was made for past wrong, and those who had been "living on the booze" began to live respectable lives through faith in the Lord Jesus.

CHAPTER IV

Remarkable Events in the Ministry of John G. Lake

In the beginning of 1909, Dr. Lake met Bishop Furze, the Bishop of the Church of England for Africa. He arranged a series of meetings for Church of England ministers to receive from the evangelist teaching along the lines of divine healing. These meetings were largly attended by ministers of this church, who came from all over the land to be present. They resulted in the establishment of the Emanuel Society for the practice of divine healing by the ministry of the Church of England in Africa. Dr. Lake tells about the results of these meetings:

THE CHALLENGE AT LOURDES, FRANCE

The meetings of this society resulted in the sending of a committee from England, of Church of England ministers to examine and report upon my work. I later accompanied that committee to England and conducted similar meetings in London for the Church of England ministers. These meetings were under the direction of Bishop Ingram, Bishop of London.

The conference authorized a committee to visit all the institutions of repute along healing lines in Europe both psychic and spiritual. In company with this committee I visited healing institutions in London. We then went to Lourdes, France. There we visited a Catholic institution where they heal by the waters of Lourdes and where they maintained a board of 200 physicians, whose business it was to examine all candidates and report upon them.

At Lourdes we also visited the greatest hypnotic institution for healing in the world. This institution sent its representatives to demonstrate their method before the Catholic Board of 200 physicians, and hearing of our committe, invited us to come before this body and give demonstrations along our lines. I agreed to take part, if I were given the final demonstration. The committee selected five candidates, people pronounced absolutely incurable. The hypnotists tried their several methods without success. I then had the five candidates placed in chairs in a row upon the platform in view of this large audience of physicians and scientists. I prayed over each one of them separately, at the same time laying my hands upon them. Three were instantly healed, a fourth recovered in a few days, and one died.

I returned to the United States for six months, holding evangelistic services in Chicago, Portland, Oakland, and Los Angeles, for the purpose of collecting a party of missionaries to take back with me to South Africa. I obtained eight men but needed $3,000 for their expenses. I had not a cent nor any in sight. While in Portland I went alone to my room and prayed for this money and received an immediate assurance that my prayer would be answered. Four days later on the night I closed my meetings in Portland, I found at my hotel a letter from George B. Studd of Los Angeles, California. I quote: "My dear Lake, There has been a windfall in your favor today. A person who does not wish to be known gave me a draft of $3,000 saying, 'God wants me to give this to Lake of South Africa. Am sending you, enclosed, therefore, a draft for $3,005, the $5 being my personal contribution."

I returned to South Africa with my missionary party in January, 1910. We went via London, England, and I preached in the church of Dr. F. B. Meyer. I visited Campbell Morgan and was invited to speak for his weekly classes as my dates prevented my filling his pulpit upon any Sunday.

In 1910 the African fever ravaged the Waterburg and Zuitkansberg districts. In less than a month, one-quarter of the black and white population died. All agencies of every character were called into action to do their best to overcome this epidemic. I went down there with assistants; four of these died. One of my nurses was sent home in a dying condition and recovered, but I never had a touch of the disease.

I never have had any kind of disease, though I have waited on and even buried people who have had the Bubonic plague — people for whom the officials offered as high as $1000 for women to nurse them. I did it without any remuneration whatever.

After studying the epidemic situation in South Africa I came to the conclusion that a special message was necessary. I went 100 miles to a telegraph station and spent $40 on a telegram to

Louis Botha, Premier of Transvaal, outlining the situation. The next day I received a telegram from him saying, "100 ox-wagons with their attendants on the road with orders to follow your instructions." (Each of these wagons were drawn by 16 oxen.)

On my return to Johannesburg, I was invited by Botha to visit Pretoria. While there, the Transvaal Parliament passed resolutions recognizing my services.

When the South African States joined together in a Union similar to those of Canada, Botha became National Premier by appointment by the King of England, who instructed him to organize a Cabinet and call elections for a Parliament. At his request, I outlined a native policy and submitted it to the Government. On receipt of this I was invited to come to Cape Town and address the Parliament on this issue. I did so — something remarkable for an American in a foreign country. I framed the policy in harmony with our American policy involving the Indian tribes, having as an example the mistakes of the United States and other nations in regard to their handling of the native nations. This policy, as outlined by me, was practically adopted by the Boer party in toto.

THE REQUEST FROM QUEEN WILHELMINA OF HOLLAND

Queen Wilhelmina of Holland entered the state of motherhood six times but was never able to carry the child to maturity. All the science of Europe could not bring the child to birth. There was a dear lady in our congregation in South Africa who had formerly been a nurse to Queen Wilhelmina. Her son was marvelously healed when dying of African fever, after he had been unconscious for six weeks.

Being a friend of the queen's, she wrote the story of her son's healing, and after some correspondence we received a written request that we pray God that she might be a real mother. I brought her letter before the congregation one Sunday night, and the congregation went down to prayer. And before I arose from my knees, I turned around and said, "All right mother, you write and tell the queen God has heard our prayer; she will bear a child." Less than a year later the child was born, the present Queen Juliana of Holland. Kings and queens are only men and women. They need the redemption of Jesus and are a mighty poor article without it.

THE MIRACLE MINISTRY OF WILLIAM T. DUGAN

One Sunday afternoon a tall Englishman walked into my church in Johannesburg, South Africa. He had a top of red hair that made him as conspicuous as a lion. He walked up the aisle and took a seat quite near the front. My old preaching partner was endeavoring to explain the mighty power of the living Christ as best he could, and this man sat listening. Presently he arose, saying, "Sir, if the things you are talking about are all right, I am your candidate."

He added, "I used to be a Christian, but I came to Africa and lived the usual African life and the result is that for three years I have been unable to do anything and my physicians say I am incurable. Tell me what to do!"

My old partner asked, "John, what shall we do?" I replied, "Call him up; we shall pray for him right now." We stepped off the platform, put our hands on William T. Dugan, and instantly — as a flash of lightning blasting a tree or rock — the power of God went through the man's being, and the Lord Jesus Christ made him well.

A few days afterward he came to my house in the middle of the day and said, "Lake, I want you to show me how to get a clean heart." I took the Word of God and went through it with him to show him the mighty, cleansing, sanctifying power of the living God in a man's heart. Before he left he knelt by a chair and consecrated his life to God.

Three months passed. One day he called and said, "I have a call from God." I knew it was. There was no mistaking it. The wonder of it was in his soul. He went down into the country where a great epidemic of fever raged. Some weeks afterward I began to receive word that people were being healed. Hundreds of them! Thousands of them! One day I concluded I would go down and join in the same work a couple of hundred miles from where he was. Somehow the news traveled to him where I was, and he came there.

The next afternoon we called at the home of a man who said his wife was sick with diabetes. We prayed for the wife and several other persons who were present. Then a man stepped out into the kitchen and asked, "Would you pray for a woman like this?" When I looked at her I saw she had club feet. The right foot was on an angle of 45 degrees and the left at right angles.

Dugan replied, "Yes. Pray for anybody." He said to her, "Sit

37

down," and taking the club foot in his hands he said, "In the name of Jesus Christ become natural." And I want to tell you that man is in the glory presence of God today and I am going to stand there with him some day. Before I had a chance to take a second breath that foot commenced to move, and the next instant that foot was straight!

Then he took up the other foot saying, "In the name of Jesus Christ become natural." Beloved, it was not the voice of the man, nor the confidence of his soul, but the mighty divine life of Jesus Christ that flashed through him and melted that foot into softness and caused it instantly to become normal by the power of God.

We have not even begun to touch the fringes of the knowledge of the power of God. However, I want to encourage your hearts. I am glad we can say what perhaps has never been said in the Christian world from the days of the apostles to the present time, that since the opening of this work in Spokane, about sixteen months ago, ten thousand people have been healed by the power of God.

Von Shield was a book agent in South Africa. He began to attend our meetings, and one day when I was not present he came forward out of the audience and knelt at the altar and sought God for a conscious knowledge of salvation. And bless God, he received it.

Some days after that when I was present and teaching at an afternoon service, he raised up in his seat and said, "Lake do you suppose that if God gave me the baptism of the Holy Spirit it would satisfy the burning yearning that is in my soul for God?" I replied, "My son, I don't know that it would, but I think it would go a long piece on the way."

So without more ado he came forward, knelt and looking up said to me, "Lay your hands on my head and pray." And as I did the Spirit of God descended in an unusual manner. He was baptized in the Holy Ghost very wonderfully indeed and became a transformed man. From that hour that man was a living personification of the power of God. All my life I have never found one through whom such majestic intense flashes of power would come at intervals as through that soul.

Presently he disappeared. His father came to me, saying, "I am troubled about Harry. He took a Bible and went off into the mountains almost three weeks ago. I am afraid he is going insane." I answered, "Brother, do not worry yourself. One of these days he will come down in the power and glory of God." I knew what was in that fellow's heart.

One day he returned under such an anointing of the Spirit as I have never before witnessed on any life. Not long after that he came to me and said, "Brother Lake, did you know this was in the Bible?" And he proceeded to read to me that familiar verse in the 16th chapter of Mark: "These signs shall follow them that believe; In my name shall they cast out devils." Looking up into my face with great earnestness, he said, "My! I wish I knew somebody that had a devil!"

AN AMAZING CASE OF DELIVERANCE

I believe God had planned that situation, for I was reminded that in my mail a couple of days before had come a request for an insane son. The mother wrote, "As far as I can tell my son has a devil," and her request was that we might come and pray that the devil might be cast out. He said, "Why this is only a couple or three blocks from where I live. I am going to find this fellow and then I am coming back for you."

I said to myself, "Here is a newborn soul, whose vision enters into the real realm of God-power." I realized that my own spirit had not touched the degree of faith that was in that soul, and I said to myself, "I do not want to say a word or do a thing that will discourage that soul in the least."

Presently he came back and said, "Brother Lake, come on." We went and found a boy who had been mad from his birth; he was like a wild animal. He would not wear clothes and would smash himself or anybody else with anything that was given him. He couldn't even have a dish from which to eat. But in the center of the enclosure where he was they had a large stone hollowed out and they would put his food in that and let him eat it just like an animal.

We tried to catch him, but he was wild as a lion. He would jump right over my head. Finally his father said, "You will not catch him out there." I had been somewhat of an athlete in my youth and I said to Von Shield, "You get on one side and if he comes to your side you will take care of him, and if he comes to my side I will take care of him."

Now beloved, this all sounds strange I know, but I'll never forget that afternoon as long as I live. As I looked across to that young man I could see the lightning flash of faith, and I knew that if he got his hands on that man the devil would come out.

Presently he landed on my side of the bed, and in an instant Von Shield sprang over the bed, laid his hands on his head and commanded the devil to come out. In two minutes that man was absolutely transformed, and was a sane man, the first moment of sanity he ever knew.

THE STRANGE CHALLENGE OF VON SHIELD

One more incident in the man's life that will help you to realize what God had done for him. The Boer people were a pioneer people. They did not have the advantages of good schools. About the only educated person in a community was the Dutch predicant. He was a real aristocrat with all the authority that the priests of Ireland exercised over the people there. One day Von Shield was conducting a service with a couple of hundred people present. The predicant was there. He arose as he was teaching and told the people that they were being misled, and that these things Von Shield was talking about were only calculated for the days of the apostles.

If Von Shield had been an ordinary young man he would have been somewhat nonplussed. But presently he said, "I will tell you how we will settle this thing. There is Miss LeRoux whom we all know. She is stone blind in one eye, and has been for four years. I will ask her to come here and I will lay hands upon her and ask the Lord Jesus to make her well." And picking up his Dutch Bible, he said to her, "And when He heals you, you will read that chapter," designating the chapter she was to read.

God Almighty met the fellow's faith; the woman's eye opened right then, and she stood before that congregation and covering the good eye, read with the eye that had been blind, the entire chapter.

40

CHAPTER V

Elias Letwaba,
the Man Who Carried on the Work

Dr. Lake returned to America in 1913 following the death of his wife. But who was to carry on this great work? God was in fact preparing a man, a humble man by the name of Elias Letwaba. The Lake story would be incomplete if we did not relate how God raised up this man to carry on the work, and of the Patmos Bible School he founded that has sent out many thousands of trained workers to evangelize Africa.

Elias Letwaba was about fourteen years of age when he was given three books by a white man who had employed him briefly as an oxen lead boy. One of the books was a dog-eared copy of the New Testament. His heart warmed as he read the story of the God of love. When he reached the age of fourteen he was scheduled to be initiated into the tribal puberty rites. These rites involved much pain. He did not shrink from that, but he felt that the vicious knowledge imparted to the boys during their initiation was wrong. When he refused to go through with it, he was looked upon as a pariah.

While some sympathized with him and would have liked to hear more about the story of Jesus, all of them feared evil spells from the witch doctors who wanted no part of Christianity.

One day a terrible flood struck that part of the country. Letwaba was standing near the river's edge, when an old man tried to cross the stream at a certain commonly used ford. But the ford had been washed out, and the old man was swept into the river. Letwaba dived in to rescue the old man and succeeded in dragging him out. When consciousness returned to the man, trembling with weakness and emotion he said, "Thank you son. God certainly sent you to rescue me."

Letwaba at that moment knew that God had called him to rescue many souls. For five years he studied the Word of God zealously, and at the same time mastered several languages.

41

Then at the age of nineteen he started out with his little brother of fourteen. It wasn't difficult for them to follow Christ's instructions that He gave to the Seventy to "carry neither purse, nor scrip, nor shoes," for they never had worn shoes, nor had they ever had more than a few pennies at a time. When he went to the first village to preach, the witch doctor expelled him. In the days which followed he suffered persecutions. He was beaten, stoned, and several times narrowly escaped death from savage animals.

Leaving the village, he went down to the river, sat on a stone and watched some bull alligators locked in a roaring battle. Suddenly he heard a group of angry men led by a scowling, powerfully built long-armed warrior coming toward him. The man looked at him for a moment and then said, "The witch doctor has sent me to kill you. Get to your feet."

"You will not kill me," Letwaba said.

"You must die," said the warrior. "Our gods the crocodiles await your coming with hungry bellies."

"Those are not gods," Letwaba said. "My God is good and all powerful. He will not permit you to slay me, for He has a work for me to do."

With that the huge servant of the witch doctor leaped at Letwaba, who had dropped to his knees in prayer. The big man missed and unable to check his rush, stumbled headlong over the kneeling man and fell into the river. The crocodiles ceased their struggle and moved toward him. Letwaba quickly waded into the river and taking hold of the warrior's foot pulled him out just as the alligators came chomping with their empty jaws.

The servant whose name was Rhino said, "Your God knocked me into the river. Why did you save me from the crocodiles?"

"Because God loves you," was the answer. The warrior quite subdued asked Letwaba to teach him about God. And for two weeks he stayed near the village explaining the New Testament to him.

For years Letwaba traveled the trails of the forest visiting hundreds of villages and kraals. Barefoot and penniless he climbed the mountains, forded the rushing streams, invaded the forest jungles to carry the message of the love of God. In some places he was received with joy; in other places he was stoned and driven away. He had thousands of converts but was unsatisfied. Somehow he felt he lacked the power he needed. After working weeks with converts in their new way of life, he would return to the village to find that many had reverted to the ways of the jungle. This gave him a feeling of guilt. He felt that somehow he was leaving something vital out of his teaching.

LETWABA MEETS DR. LAKE

It was about this time that Letwaba came in contact with Dr. Lake and his partner Tom Hezmelhalch. In the very first meeting a mighty faith began to rise in the young man's breast. He said to himself, "At last I am to find that for which I have longed."

But he was hardly prepared for what he was to see. He had never dared to hope to witness such demonstrations of divine power. There was a love, a heavenliness, an all-embracing tenderness to which Letwaba had been a stranger. He had been accompanied to the meetings by friends, and to one of these, on the way, he confided his great yearnings of heart as follows: "John Muruani, if I do not get what I want now, I shall die. My soul simply cries out for a real victory over sin. I am tired of seeing ministers drinking and smoking, while at the same time preaching the gospel. Better that we leave religion rather than continue preaching while at the same time living a powerless, sinful life. I don't want theory. I want reality. I want God."

And the seeker found what he wanted. Lake put his arm about the black man's neck and kissed him, calling him "My brother," while many of the unconverted white men in the hall booed and hissed at him, shouting, "Bah! Fancy kissing a black man! He may be your brother but he's not mine," and similar expressions of disapproval and contempt.

Lake turned on the crowd like a flash, and shouted, "My friends, God has made of one blood all nations of men!' (Acts 17:26). If you don't want to acknowledge them as your brothers, then you'll have the mortification of going away into eternal woe, while you see many of these black folk going to eternal bliss. 'Whosoever hateth his brother is a murderer: and ye know that no murderer hath eternal life abiding in him'!" (I John 3:15).

Then holding out his hand to Letwaba once more, he said, "Brother, I'm glad to welcome you into our midst."

The furore and hissing increased, and many shouted, "Put out the black devils. Kick them into the street."

However Lake, with his hand still upon Letwaba's shoulder,

43

said quite calmly, "If you turn out these men, then you must turn me out, too, for I will stand by my black brethren."

Letwaba was accustomed to insult and reproach. Indeed every black man in South Africa had been made to feel it more or less. But such love, such uncompromising conviction and speech from a white preacher were absolutely new to him; and it won his heart, while at the same time it subdued the gainsayers until they sank into a sullen silence.

In the course of the meeting Letwaba noticed the liberty of the Spirit. It is true that the leaders kept a quiet, firm hold of proceedings, but anyone who was moved by the Spirit had the opportunity to speak, testify, give messages in tongues or prophesy.

God confirmed His Word with new signs and wonders in every meeting. Thus a young man, under the power of the Spirit and with eyes closed and arms uplifted, rose from his seat and went to stand over a complete stranger, a man with stiff, upstanding, red hair. He prayed over him, and said, "Man! God is calling you for His service."

The stranger got up, evidently in a towering rage, and stamped out of the meeting. The young man cried, "God bring him back, and help him to obey Thee."

Shortly afterwards this man returned, was saved and filled with the Holy Spirit.

A lady came up to Lake and said, "I long for God, but I cannot stand the life I am living at present. My husband is a drunken profligate. I shall have to leave him."

Lake replied, "Madam! You cannot show me any scriptural sanction for leaving your husband. Rather let us pray for him."

They knelt and prayed, and as they pleaded with God the power of the Spirit fell upon this poor heartbroken woman, and she found herself praising God in tongues, while the sisters who surrounded her and prayed with her soon felt in their souls the assurance that God was answering prayer for the drunken husband.

The woman went home, and to her sorrow found her husband still drunken, quarrelsome and noisy. She sank onto her bed in grief and fell asleep. Later on awakening, to her amazement she saw her husband kneeling beside the bed, crying to God for mercy and salvation. To the end of his days that man's

44

conversion proved real, and he was one of the most humble and most used workers of the band during the days that followed.

Letwaba had never seen such amazing conversions, such mighty miracles, such uncompromising teaching for holiness and against sin. He could not help feeling, "These people are living what they preach. They not only talk about it, but they have the experience of it."

Thus he went to Lake's private house for further enlightenment. There he made a full breast of all his past life: his failures, his longings, his powerlessness, while Lake showed him the way of deliverance through taking one's part in the death and resurrection of Christ and through a daily putting to death of the deeds of the flesh. Letwaba longed to hear more of all this. It was as water to one who had been slowly dying of thirst.

Brothers Lake and Hezmelhalch were about to leave for Bleomfontein, and so Letwaba joined the party. There, on February 9th, 1909, he was filled with the Holy Spirit and praised and magnified God in new tongues, just as the saints have done from the earliest days of the Christian Church. He was simply overcome by the power of God till his whole being was aflame, and he realized that at last the longing of his heart was satisfied.

He could declare, as could the first apostolic band in Acts 2:16, "This is that which was spoken by the prophet Joel." It was not some poor man-made counterfeit, some miserable ecclesiastical makeshift, but the Holy Spirit of God Himself had come to take up His abode in His human temple.

Letwaba had received power from on high: that power without which every pastor and minister is cold and inefficient, whatever his theological training or mental ability may be. God has never yet given any substitute for the power of the Holy Ghost.

One thing struck Letwaba very forcibly: There was never any rigid programme in the meetings, but God was always doing some new and marvelous thing. At times a town hall would be hired. At other places religious bigotry closed every public building to this party of Spirit-filled saints, and they had to hold their services in private houses, but everywhere they showed love for hate, good for evil.

Sometimes an amazing prophecy would be fulfilled before the eyes of the people. At other times the new tongues given and interpreted would be recognized by someone present. Frequently those converted became earnest workers. Baptismal services were large and frequent. The very fact that so many churches spoke and argued against the work merely served as an advertisement.

One night when Tom Hezmelhalch was preaching in English in the home of Mr. and Mrs. Stuart, at Krugersdorp, a Zulu servant, who did not understand English, yet came under conviction of sin, was soundly converted. He had understood everything that was preached, it being revealed to him by the Holy Spirit just as though it had been preached in his own language. That night at ten o'clock he came back to the house saying, "God told me to come back for more prayer."

Before long this Zulu servant fell under the power of the Spirit, and left the house praising the Lord in new tongues.

From that time onward Mr. and Mrs. Stuart declare that he was a splendid servant: always willing and keen to obey. His work was done conscientiously, and one could rest assured that anything he undertook would be accomplished to the very best of his ability, not for money's sake but because it was done for Christ. Moreover, when this servant had any spare time he would go out preaching the gospel to his fellows, and praying for the sick, so that very many were brought to Christ through his testimony.

It was by such remarkable and unexpected means that God opened fresh doors for the Lake party, and as Letwaba watched, he saw at last the difference between working on mere man-planned lines and being led by the Holy Spirit.

CHAPTER VI

The Mantle Falls on Letwaba

Letwaba now realized a new victory in his life, that he had never experienced before. His heart was filled with joy. His first convert was his own father who had been seeking further light. He too received the baptism of the Holy Ghost. From then on Letwaba began to preach with great power and unction. Naturally this drew upon him a storm of persecution. He was stoned, beaten, kicked, shouted down, and insulted. Yet he would get up again, and go his way preaching and telling the good news of what God had done for him and could do for others. He manifested such love to his persecutors that often their railings and curses turned to wonderment, and many times to a saving knowledge of Christ.

Letwaba prevailed upon the American missionaries to go northward with him with plans for the evangelization of Northern Transvaal. Unfortunately the missionaries were not acclimated to the severe hardships and unhealthful conditions of the interior and found it physically impossible to continue. They were forced to return South before their mission could be completed. Letwaba was broken-hearted over this; his hopes and anticipations had risen so high in the visit of the missionaries. Now they had come and gone, and he was left to struggle on alone. Yet although he knew it not, God was preparing him to do this very work, and he was to be the shepherd to these countrymen of his, scattered over the remote reaches of Northern Transvaal.

Since those upon whom Letwaba had set such hopes had left forever from the Transvaal field, he looked to God as to what should be done next. Gradually the Lord showed him that he was the very one that was to carry this message of deliverance to his countrymen. Thus it came about that Letwaba began his ministry in Northern Transvaal. He was to walk many hundreds of weary miles, along dusty roads, and twisting paths, and through tangled thorn-tree scrub, preaching the message of deliverance. It wasn't easy going, and sometimes the natives were hostile. At other times large crowds gathered to hear him. But it was his ministry of miracles that really opened the doors to him.

In one native village he found the people almost in a panic. Rain had not fallen in a long time, draught had ruined the crops, and the spectre of famine stalked the land. The witch doctors began to talk about making horrible sacrifices to the rain-god. They spoke defiantly of the white man's God and his inability to bring rain. Into this desperate situation Letwaba walked. Letwaba called upon those who would listen to him, to repent, that they might have reasonable and Scriptural grounds to rest their faith. Then he had a mighty inspiration. As he preached, the power of a great anointing came upon him. Words came clearly and rapidly and the people listened spellbound. Then Letwaba told them, "Do you not know that whatever believers bind on earth is bound in heaven, and what we loose on earth is loosed in heaven? Do you know that we have authority to ask what we will, and it shall be granted in the name of Jesus? I declare to you people, by the Word of the Lord, that by this time tomorrow you shall have the rain that you need. Your fields and your cattle shall be saved, and you shall know that God still lives to answer the prayers of those who believe in Him."

It was a challenge that Elijah the prophet might have made. The people gathered off in groups to discuss what Letwaba had said. Some scoffed and sneered. Others said, "We shall wait to see if his words are true."

It had been easy for Letwaba to give forth the message when the anointing was upon him. But in the afternoon, when the people had dispersed, a great trembling took hold of him. Above him the sky was brass. Not a cloud was in the sky. The sun beat down with a pitiless heat, while about him cattle stood disconsolately trying to grub up roots where grass had been. Awful thoughts took hold of Letwaba. "What if on the morrow, rain should not come? What would the witch doctors say then? What would the people think? What of those who had hung on to his words with a desperate hope?" He would be considered a false prophet making sport at their expense. These thoughts rushed like a torrent through Letwaba's brain.

The preacher went up into the mountains to be alone with God. It was night and the stars came out. It looked as if his entire ministry were at stake on the issue of events of the morrow. It was Letwaba's Gethsemane. On through the night he pleaded with God. "Not for the sake of my reputation, Lord but lest the heathen should belittle Thy name and spurn Thy Word." Morning came and with it the breaking of a cloudless day. But the answer was at hand.

With startling suddenness clouds massed up, and by the time that Letwaba returned to the village he was drenched to the skin. It will not require any imagination on the reader's part to realize that with the breaking of the drought the hearts of the people were opened now to the Gospel that Letwaba preached. Lake had known nights of prayer in wrestling against the powers of darkness. Letwaba too had learned the lesson of prevailing prayer which gives men power with God and then power with men.

Once Lake was called to the bedside of a boy that was dying of a broken neck, the result of an accident. Lake took Letwaba along with him and together they pleaded for the healing of the native lad. Night came and the answer did not come. Brother Lake said, "His neck is gone, his spine is broken." Letwaba answered, "It doesn't matter what is broken. God will answer if we trust Him." At this time Dr. Lake left to go to the place where they were being entertained.

About three o'clock in the morning Letwaba entered, and Lake asked, "How is the boy?" Letwaba answered, "Praise God, prayer is answered, and Jesus' name is vindicated. The lad is strong and well."

The time came when John Lake and Tom Hezmelhalch left Africa to return to America. But the seeds planted continued to grow. Other native workers as Letwaba carried the message from one end of the land to the other. The greatest handicap was their lack of knowledge of the Word, which often resulted in their being carried off into unbalanced teaching and fanaticism. This was illustrated in the case of Edward Lyons, in Basutoland.

Lyons was saved and had a wonderful experience of the Baptism of the Holy Ghost. He was able to gather crowds to hear him of five and six thousand. Sometimes he would preach all day, then he would pray for the sick. Thousands were miraculously made whole. At times he would pray all night, until he would have to say, "Friends, I can pray no more, but Jesus has said, 'The works that I do shall he do also; and greater works than these shall he do.' Do you not see that there is no limit to what can be done in Jesus' name? Thus I sit on this stone in Jesus' name, and after doing so, go off to sleep. But I am leaving my helpers to direct the sick to the stone, that there may be no panic or crushing of each other. Come quietly, in line, and sit on the stone on which I have sat, and you shall get healed in Jesus' name." All through the night the long queue of sick would move past the stone, and as each sat upon it, he, or she would leap up with shouts of praise to God for healing.

Unfortunately in the absence of spiritually mature teachers, Lyons got into error and gave fanciful and absurb prophecies which soon resulted in his being discredited, Exaltation of self had taken the place of Christ and the result was shame and confusion.

THE MANTLE FALLS ON LETWABA

Letwaba saw this, and felt that there was a great need that the native preachers should be taught the Word. Thus came the idea of building a Bible School. With no funds nor hope of outside aid, he nevertheless believed that God would enable him to accomplish his vision in this respect. The most fanatical absurdities were liable to occur unless the ministers could be taught the Word.

Indeed African religious history is filled with cases of mass reversion or backsliding. One such example is the French Cameroons where Africa's earliest missionaries converted the entire population, established churches and tribal congregations. Yet today witchcraft is more pervasive than it ever was. This is understandable to one who knows the primitive African mind. There is a simplicity about them; they are very impressionable to forces whether evil or good. To them there is only one cure to the infinitude of epidemics, disasters and famines that plague the African tribesmen — counter spells by the witch doctors.

In view of these things, what was Letwaba to do? What could strip from the lives of these men their fear of evil spells, their superstitions, their dread of arousing the enmity of the witch doctors and cleanse them of the jungle heart? The ministry of John G. Lake had given him the clue. The answer was found in Matthew 10:1.

> "And when he had called unto him his twelve disciples, he gave them power against unclean spirits, to cast them out, and to heal all manner of sickness and all manner of disease."

50

Letwaba went through the New Testament and jotted down all the Scriptures on healing. He went to some white ministers for further help, but one said, "True, Letwaba, Jesus healed the sick when He was on earth, but when He died, the days of miracles passed with Him." Another said, "I think God might still heal the sick if one had sufficient faith. But who in these days has such faith?"

But Letwaba had seen the miraculous in the Lake meetings. He gave himself to prayer. All night he looked to God, and when the morning light came they saw him still kneeling, his face alight with great happiness. "God has spoken," he said. And he handed his friend a note on which he had written, "Jesus Christ the same yesterday, and today, and forever" (Heb. 13:8). "For I am the Lord, I change not" (Mal. 3:6).

Now more than ever Letwaba felt the need to preach the Gospel. He read those words, "Go ye into all the world, and preach the gospel to every creature" (Mark 16:15). But one thing troubled him. Winning souls was one thing, but keeping them true to God was another. He had seen so much backsliding that his heart reached out for the answer. While he was praying about this, his eyes lit upon II Tim. 2:2. With an almost overpowering sense of awe he read:

"And the things that thou hast heard of me among many witnesses, the same commit thou to faithful men, who shall be able to teach others also."

Suddenly he realized that God was talking to him. God was saying, "You must start a Bible School, O Letwaba." But where would he get the money to build a school? He was sure that God would help him, but first he felt he must develop the ministry of healing that God had revealed to him. He said, "I must go on a journey, for I am filled with fire to tell the people that God is the Healer of the body as well as the soul."

Those were two marvelous years. Barefoot and hatless he wandered far to the mountain tribes, to the fever-ridden natives of Rhodesia, to the disease-plagued Basutos, and other tribes. He spoke to the poor and to the great chieftains. Praying for the sick opened the hearts of the people to his message of salvation. It was a marvelous story. More than ten thousand sick were permanently healed and over a hundred thousand souls were led to Christ.

To those people Letwaba promised a Bible School. He felt

he must train teachers who would be able to explain the Bible intelligently and properly direct young men so that they would not fall into the fanatical absurdities that so often occurred among primitive people.

The matter of the Bible School had been the object of constant prayer during those two years. He knew he would need land and timber and food for the students, for few of the students and their families had any money at all. After his return to Potgietersrus, he gave himself to a night of prayer. Then he went to the town council and they promptly gave him enough land for his project. He announced a dedication service for the land, and people came from great distances. Among them he noted many members of mobs who had beaten him years before, and his voice was momentarily choked by tears.

Following his prayer a farmer came up and gave him all the timber that he would need. Two natives stepped up who had experience in sawing and said, "We will saw your timber without pay, except sufficient corn meal for our porridge." In fact people everywhere promised to help. So it was within a year two dormitories were built, one for men and one for women. A small farm was given him, and the food problem was chiefly solved.

Today many thousands of graduates from the Patmos Bible School are teaching and preaching the Gospel throughout Africa. Every graduate is deeply spiritual and chosen for his love of God and mankind. The study of the Bible is emphasized, and when the students go forth, they go armed with the Gospel of Truth. And so Letwaba as no other man carried on the great work started by John G. Lake in Africa. It is still going on today.

CHAPTER VII

The Return to America

When John G. Lake departed Africa after five years of ministry, he left behind 125 white congregations and 500 native ones. Although he possessed a strong constitution, the strain of the work plus the responsibility of caring for a large family made it necessary for him to return to America.

Late in the year of 1913 he was married to Miss Florence Switzer. In the summer of 1914 while walking on the street he met his old friend James Hill, the railroad magnate.

"Where are you going?" asked Hill.

"I really don't know," I said. "I am wandering around trying to gather health, and preaching as I go."

"Come to my office," continued Mr. Hill. Upon arriving there, he turned to his clerk and said, "Make out passes for Mr. Lake and his wife, good over all our lines." Then turning to me, he added, "And when they run out, send for more."

With these passes Dr. Lake went to Spokane. After looking around he decided to set up healing rooms in the city. The ministry during the next five or six years in that city has rarely been equalled in the history of the Church. It is estimated that some 100,000 healings occurred during that time.

In fact the reports of miracles of healing became so numerous that eventually a Committee from the Better Business Bureau was chosen to investigate the truthfulness of all the public announcements appearing in the city papers. For some time previous the church had been publishing some of the wonderful testimonies of healing by the power of God that had taken place in the daily course of the ministry at the Divine Healing Institute.

The testimonies were so astounding that many complaints had reached the Better Business Bureau to the effect that the testimonies must certainly be untrue. The Better Business Bureau promptly undertook an investigation, and their call at the Healing Rooms was for that purpose.

In the presence of the committee, Dr. Lake called in 18 persons whose testimonies had appeared in public print. They in turn gave testimony of their own condition and the wonder of their healing by the power of God in the name of the Lord Jesus Christ under this ministry. After 18 had been examined, Dr. Lake presented them with names of many healed persons in the city, desiring them to go personally to these persons and investigate for themselves whether these things be so.

He then suggested to the committee that on Sunday, June 23 at three o'clock in the afternoon, at their public service, they would present 100 cases of healed persons for their investigation and invited them to form a committee composed of physicians, lawyers, judges, educators and businessmen who should render a verdict.

In the days lapsing between the interview at the Healing Rooms and Sunday, June 23, the committee continued their investigation, interviewing persons whose names he had furnished them. On Friday, June 21, before the great Sunday meeting, Dr. Lake received a letter from the committee assuring him that they had no desire in any way to interfere with the good which Dr. Lake was doing, and gently let themselves down so that their appearance at the Sunday meeting would not be necessary. Two members of the committee saw the pastor privately and said that the committee was astounded. They said, "We soon found out upon investigation, you did not tell half of it."

Although the committee had given notice of their withdrawal from the investigation, Dr. Lake announced that the meeting would be held as planned and that he would appeal to the public for a verdict. The meeting took place at the Masonic Temple before a large audience estimated by the police to number thousands, hundreds being compelled to stand throughout the entire service and hundreds were refused admittance.

Dr. Lake gave a brief statement on the reasons for the meeting and of the desire to glorify God by permitting the city and the world to know that Jesus had never changed, that prayer was answerable today as it ever was, and the days of miracles had not passed, but were forever possible through exercise of faith in God.

Following this many testimonies were given. We can give only a few which were typical of many:

Rev. R. Armstrong, a Methodist minister, of N.2819 Colum-

54

bus Avenue, healed of sarcoma growing out of the left shoulder three times as large as a man's head, was healed in answer to prayer.

Rev. Thomas B. O'Reilly of 430 Rookery Building, testified to being healed of seizures so violent that when stricken with them it required seven policemen to overpower and confine him in the hospital, of his instantaneous healing and perfect restoration to health through the prayer of faith.

Baby Agnes Young, N.169 Post Street, healed of extreme malnutrition; patient at the Deaconess Hospital for nine months, from the time of birth until her healing. She weighed six-and-a-half pounds at birth and at the age of nine months, only four-and-a half pounds. One evening when one of the ministers from Rev. Lake's Healing Rooms called to minister to her, she was found in the dead room; the nurse, believing her to be dead, had removed her to the dead room. He took the child in his arms, praying the prayer of faith; God heard and answered, removed her from the hospital and placed her in the hands of a Christian woman for nursing. In six weeks she was perfectly well and strong. The father and mother arose to corroborate the testimony. They are both members of Dr. Lake's church.

Mrs. Everetts, 1811 Boone Avenue, testified to her healing of varicose veins. She had suffered from them for 38 years. The veins were enlarged until they were the size of goose eggs in spots. Under the right knee there was a sack of blood so large that the knee was made stiff. She had exhausted every medical method. After being ministered to at the Healing Rooms for a short period, she was entirely well and the veins are perfectly clear.

Mrs. Constance Hoag, Puyallup, Washington, broke her knee cap. A section of the bone protruded through the flesh. She wrote requesting that the ministers of the Healing Rooms lay their hands upon a handkerchief in faith and prayer and send it to her, in accordance with Acts 19:12. This was done. She applied the handkerchief to the knee and in 15 minutes the pain had gone, and in an hour the bone had returned to place and was perfectly healed.

Mrs. Walker, Granby Court, was an invalid at the Deaconess Hospital from internal cancer; after an exploratory operation, was pronounced incurable by the doctors. She also had a severe case of neuritis. Her suffering was unspeakable. She testified to her healing and of her restoration to perfect health, the cancer having passed from her body in seven sections. Since then many have been healed through her prayer and faith.

Mrs. John A. Graham, E.369 Hartson, a nurse and hospital matron, was operated on for fibroid tumor. The generative organs were removed, and at a later date was operated on a second time for gallstones. The operation not being a success, she was eventually left to die. In the throes of death and unconsciousness, she was healed by the power of God in answer to prayer of one of the ministers called from the Healing Rooms. The organs that had been removed in the operation re-grew in the body and she became a normal woman and a mother. (Wonderful applause.)

Mrs. Wolverton was injured in a Great Northern railroad wreck and was awarded large damages by the court. Physicians testified her injuries to be such that motherhood was impossible. After her marriage the physicians' testimony was confirmed. She was healed in answer to prayer and gave birth to a son, and since has given birth to twins.

Mrs. Lamphear, 115½ Sprague Avenue, was an invalid for 11 years, suffering from prolapsus of the stomach, bowels and uterus, also from tuberculosis and rheumatism. Her husband carried her from place to place in his arms. After 11 years of terrible suffering, upon the advice of her physicians who were unable to assist her, she was sent to Soap Lake, Oregon, for bath treatments. Ordinary baths had no effect on her and the superintendent testified that they had finally placed her in super-heated baths, hotter than any in which they had ever before put a human being. Through this treatment an abnormal growth was started in the left leg and foot. Her leg became three inches longer than the other and her foot one inch too long. A bone as large as an orange grew on the knee. She received an instant healing of rheumatism. The leg shortened at the rate of an inch a week, the foot also shortened to its normal length and the bone growth on the knee totally disappeared. Her tuberculosis was healed, and she is praising God for His goodness. Born without the outer lobe on her ear, it also grew on.

Mrs. Carter, of S.714 Sherman Street, wife of Policeman Carter, was examined by seven physicians who pronounced her to be suffering from a fibroid tumor, estimated to weigh 15 pounds. She was ministered to at the Healing Rooms at 4:30 in the afternoon and at 11 o'clock the next day returned to the

Healing Rooms perfectly healed and wearing her corset, the enormous tumor having dematerialized.

Mr. John Dewitt of Granby Court, testified on behalf of Frederick Barnard, 32 years of age, who was injured in his babyhood from a fall from a baby cab, causing curvature of the spine. As he grew to boyhood and manhood he was never able to take part in the sports common to boyhood and manhood. When the great war came on, he would stand around the recruiting offices, covetously watching the men who enlisted for the war. One day he expressed to Mr. Dewitt the sorrow of his soul that he was not able to enlist also. Mr. Dewitt told him of Mr. Lake's Healing Rooms and invited him to come and be ministered to. The curvature of his spine straightened and his height increased an inch. He applied for enlistment in the Canadian army and was accepted by the army physician as first class and sent abroad.

Now comes one of the most remarkable cases in history. The Risdon family stand holding their six-year-old son on their shoulders. This boy was born with a closed head. In consequence, as he increased in years, the skull was forced upward like the roof of a house, the forehead and the back of the head also being forced out in similar manner, giving the head the appearance of the hull of a yacht upside down. The pressure on the brain caused the right side to become paralyzed and the child was dumb. Physicians said that nothing could be done for him until he was 12 years old, and then the entire top of the head would have to be removed, the sides of the skull expanded, and the entire head covered with a silver plate. Under Divine Healing ministration in answer to prayer the bones softened, the head expanded, the skull was reduced to its normal size, the paralysis disappeared, the dumbness was gone. He spoke like other children and afterwards attended the public school.

Remarks by Rev. Lake: "I want you to see that in the Spirit of God there is a science far beyond physical or psychological science and the man or woman who enters into the spirit relation with God and exercises His power is most scientific; that the power of God in this instance was sufficient to soften the bones of the head, expand the skull and bring the head down to normal when the child was four-and-a-half years old — something that no medicine could do and no surgical operation could accomplish without endangering the life of the child."

Mrs. Lena Lakey, W. 116 Riverside Avenue, testified of having suffered with violent insanity. She was a cook at a lumber camp. She told of the men at the camp endeavoring to overpower her and tie her in the bed; of her tearing the bed to pieces and breaking her arms free; of how she struck one man with the side of the bed, rendering him unconscious. Another was in the hospital three weeks recovering from injuries. She escaped into the woods in a drenching rain, eventually falling exhausted in a copse of trees, where she lay unconscious for six hours until a searching party found her. She was brought to Spokane in an auto by six men and was tied with ropes. Before taking her to the court to be committed to the insane asylum they decided to take her to the Healing Rooms. Rev. Lake laid his hands on her in prayer, and the demons were cast out and she was instantly healed. An abscess in her side from which she had suffered for 15 years totally disappeared in 24 hours, and a rheumatic bone deposit between the joints of the fingers and toes, so extensive that it forced the joint apart, was gone in 48 hours. She was made every whit whole.

Addressing the audience, Mr. Lake said: "All persons who have been healed by the power of God and who desire to add their testimony to these who have already been given, stand." Two hundred and sixty-seven persons arose. While they stood Mr. Lake said: "Gentlemen of the committee and audience, you see these witnesses; you have heard the testimonies. Gentlemen of the committee and audience, has this been a fair presentation?" (Shouts of "Yes, Yes" from all parts of the house.) "Did God heal these people?" (Cries of "Yes, Yes.") "Is divine healing a fact?" (Replies from audience, "It surely is.") "Gentlemen of the committee and audience are you entirely satisfied?" (Replies from the audience, "Indeed we are.")

The services then closed with the prayer of consecration, spoken clause by clause by the Rev. Lake and repeated by the audience.